INDIAN RECIPES 2021

FLAVORFUL INDIAN RECIPES

TALA GREENE

Table of Contents

Turnip Pickle

Ingredients

250g/9oz turnips, chopped into 2.5cm/1in pieces

240ml/6fl oz water

120ml/¼fl oz refined vegetable oil

8 garlic cloves, crushed

1 tbsp ginger paste

240ml/6fl oz malt vinegar

125g/4½oz jaggery*,

grated

1 tsp chilli powder

4 cloves

5cm/2in cinnamon

2 green cardamom pods

1 tsp mustard seeds, ground

1 tbsp salt

Method

- Boil the turnips with the water on a low heat for 15 minutes. Drain and set aside.

- Heat the oil in a saucepan. Fry the garlic and the ginger paste on a low heat till golden brown.
- Add the boiled turnip and all the remaining ingredients. Mix well.
- Cook the mixture until the oil separates.
- Cool and transfer to a clean, dry jar.

NOTE: *This can be stored in a refrigerator for a month.*

Sweet Mango Pickle

Ingredients

500g/1lb 2oz unripe mangoes, peeled and finely sliced

Salt to taste

1 tsp turmeric

120ml/4fl oz refined vegetable oil

2 cloves

2.5cm/1in cinnamon

6 black peppercorns

1 tsp chilli powder

250g/9oz grated jaggery*

5cm/2in root ginger, finely sliced

12 garlic cloves, finely sliced

Method

- Rub the mango slices with the salt and turmeric. Set aside for an hour.
- Squeeze out water by pressing the mango slices between your palms. Set aside.
- Heat the oil in a saucepan. Add the cloves, cinnamon and peppercorns.
- Let them splutter for 15 seconds. Add the mango slices and mix well.

- Add the chilli powder, jaggery, ginger and garlic. Mix well and cook over a low heat till the jaggery melts into a thick syrup.
- Allow the pickle to cool. Store in a dry, clean jar and keep aside for a day.

NOTE: *This can be stored in the refrigerator for a month.*

Carrot Pickle

Ingredients

6½ tbsp refined vegetable oil

1 tsp mustard seeds

1 tsp fenugreek seeds

½ tsp asafoetida

1 tsp turmeric

2 tsp chilli powder

Salt to taste

250g/9oz carrots, thinly sliced

Method

- Heat the oil in a saucepan. Add the mustard seeds, fenugreek seeds, asafoetida, turmeric, chilli powder and the salt. Fry on a low heat for 15 seconds.
- Allow the mixture to cool. Pour over the carrot slices and let stand for 2-3 hours.
- Store in a clean, dry jar.

NOTE: *This can be stored in the refrigerator for a week.*

Green Coconut Chutney

Ingredients

200g/7oz coriander leaves

100g/3½oz grated fresh coconut

2 green chillies

8 garlic cloves

Salt to taste

60ml/2fl oz water

Method

- Grind all the ingredients together. Store in a clean, dry jar.

NOTE: *This can be stored in the refrigerator for 2-3 days.*

Mint Chutney

Ingredients

100g/3½oz fresh mint leaves

1 large onion

3 green chillies

8 garlic cloves

Salt to taste

1 tbsp water

Method

- Grind all the ingredients together. Store in a clean, dry jar for 2-3 days.

Peanut Chutney

Ingredients

250g/9oz roasted peanuts

1 tsp chilli powder

2 tsp sugar

Salt to taste

Method

- Grind all the ingredients together. Store in a clean, dry jar for 10 days.

Papaya Chutney

Ingredients

1 tsp salt

2 tsp sugar

200g/7oz grated unripe papaya

2 tbsp refined vegetable oil

1 tsp cumin seeds

8 curry leaves

3 green chillies, slit lengthways

½ tsp turmeric

Method

- Mix the salt and the sugar with the grated papaya. Set aside.
- Heat the oil in a saucepan. Add the cumin seeds, curry leaves, green chillies and turmeric. Let them splutter for 15 seconds.
- Pour this over the grated papaya mixture. Mix well.
- Allow the mixture to cool and then store in a clean, dry jar.

NOTE: *This can be stored in the refrigerator for a week.*

Sweet & Sour Mango Pickle

Ingredients

500g/1lb 2oz unripe mangoes, peeled and chopped into 5cm/2in strips

Salt to taste

125g/4½oz mustard seeds, coarsely ground

3 tbsp water

180g/6½oz grated jaggery*

1 tsp chilli powder

1½ tbsp refined vegetable oil

1 tsp mustard seeds

½ tsp asafoetida

½ tsp turmeric

Method

- Rub the mango slices with salt. Set aside.
- Mix the ground mustard with half a tsp of salt and the water.
- Mix this well with the mango slices, along with the jaggery and chilli powder.
- Heat the oil in a saucepan. Add the mustard seeds, asafoetida and turmeric. Let them splutter for 15 seconds.

- Remove from the heat and pour this oil over the mango mixture. Mix thoroughly.
- Allow to cool and store in a clean, dry jar.

NOTE: *This can be stored in the refrigerator for a month.*

Aubergine Pickle

Ingredients

120ml/4fl oz refined vegetable oil

1 tsp mustard seeds

1 tsp fenugreek seeds

2 tsp ground cumin

2.5cm/1in root ginger, finely chopped

12 garlic cloves, finely chopped

4 green chillies, finely chopped

500g/1lb 2oz aubergine, chopped into 2.5cm/1in pieces

125g/4½oz sugar

120ml/4fl oz malt vinegar

Salt to taste

Method

- Heat the oil in a saucepan. Add the mustard seeds, fenugreek seeds and ground cumin.
- Let them splutter for 15 seconds. Add the ginger, garlic and green chillies. Fry on a low heat for a minute.
- Add the aubergine pieces. Mix well to coat with the oil. Cook for 3-4 minutes on a medium heat, stirring well.
- Add the sugar, vinegar and the salt. Cook over a low heat till the aubergine pieces become soft. Allow any extra liquid to evaporate.
- Remove from the heat and cool.
- Store in a clean, dry jar.

NOTE: *This can be stored in the refrigerator for a month.*

Curry Leaves Dry Pickle

Ingredients

25g/scant 1oz curry leaves, dry roasted

250g/9oz kaala chana*, roasted

1 tbsp sugar

8 dry red chillies

Salt to taste

Method

- Dry grind all the ingredients together.
- Store in a clean, dry jar.

NOTE: *This can be stored in the refrigerator for a month.*

Tomato Pickle

Ingredients

240ml/6fl oz refined vegetable oil

1 tsp mustard seeds

¼ tsp fenugreek seeds

1 tsp cumin seeds

½ tsp turmeric

8 curry leaves

2 tsp ginger paste

2 tsp garlic paste

2 red chillies, slit lengthways

4 tomatoes, blanched, skinned and chopped

250ml/8fl oz malt vinegar

250g/9oz sugar

Salt to taste

Method

- Heat the oil in a saucepan. Add the mustard seeds, fenugreek seeds, cumin seeds, turmeric, curry leaves, ginger paste, garlic paste and the red chillies. Fry for 30 seconds.
- Add the tomatoes. Mix well.
- Add the vinegar, sugar and salt. Cook on a low heat for 20 minutes.
- Remove from the heat and allow the mixture to cool. Store in clean, dry jar.

NOTE: *This can be stored in the refrigerator for a month.*

Crunchy Spinach Patty

Makes 12

Ingredients

1 tbsp refined vegetable oil plus extra for deep frying

1 large onion, finely chopped

50g/1¾oz spinach, boiled and finely chopped

1 tsp garlic paste

1 tsp ginger paste

Salt to taste

300g/10oz paneer*, chopped

2 eggs, whisked

2 tbsp plain white flour

Pepper to taste

Salt to taste

50g/1¾oz breadcrumbs

Method

- Heat the oil in a frying pan. Fry the onion on a medium heat till translucent.
- Add the spinach, garlic paste, ginger paste and salt. Cook for 2-3 minutes.

- Remove from the heat and add the paneer. Mix well and divide into square patties. Cover with foil and refrigerate for 30 minutes.
- Mix the eggs, flour, pepper and salt together to form a smooth batter.
- Heat the remaining oil in a frying pan. Dip each paneer patty into the batter, roll in the breadcrumbs and deep fry till golden brown.
- Serve hot with dry garlic chutney

Rava Dosa

(Semolina Crêpe)

Makes 10-12

Ingredients

100g/3½oz semolina

85g/3oz plain white flour

Pinch of bicarbonate of soda

250g/9oz yoghurt

240ml/8fl oz water

Salt to taste

Refined vegetable oil for greasing

Method

- Blend all the ingredients, except the oil, together to form a batter of a pancake-mix consistency. Set aside for 20-30 minutes.
- Grease and heat a flat pan. Pour 2 tbsp of batter in it. Spread by lifting the pan and rotating it gently.
- Pour some oil around the edges.
- Cook for 3 minutes. Flip and cook till crisp.
- Repeat for the remaining batter.
- Serve hot with coconut chutney

Doodhi Cutlet

(Bottle Gourd Cutlet)

Makes 20

Ingredients

1 tbsp refined vegetable oil plus extra for frying

1 large onion, chopped

4 green chillies, finely chopped

2.5cm/1in root ginger, grated

1 large bottle gourd*, peeled and grated

Salt to taste

2 eggs, whisked

100g/3½oz breadcrumbs

For the white sauce:

2 tbsp margarine/butter

4 tbsp flour

Salt to taste

Pepper to taste

1 tbsp cream

Method

- For the white sauce, heat the margarine/butter in a saucepan.
  Add all the remaining white sauce ingredients and stir on a medium heat till thick and creamy. Set aside.
- Heat the oil in a frying pan. Fry the onion, green chillies and ginger on a medium heat for 2-3 minutes.
- Add the bottle gourd and salt. Mix well. Cover with a lid and cook for 15-20 minutes on a medium heat.
- Uncover and mash the bottle gourd well. Add the white sauce and half the whisked eggs. Set aside for 20 minutes to harden and set.
- Chop the mixture into cutlets.
- Heat the oil in a saucepan. Dip each cutlet in the remaining whisked egg, roll in the breadcrumbs and deep fry till golden brown.
- Serve hot with sweet tomato chutney

Patra

(Colocasia Leaf Pinwheel)

Makes 20

Ingredients

10 colocasia leaves*

2 tbsp refined vegetable oil

½ tsp mustard seeds

1 tsp sesame seeds

1 tsp cumin seeds

8 curry leaves

2 tbsp coriander leaves, finely chopped

For the batter:

250g/9oz besan*

4 tbsp jaggery*, grated

1 tsp tamarind paste

½ tsp ginger paste

½ tsp garlic paste

1 tsp chilli powder

½ tsp turmeric

Salt to taste

Method

- Mix all the batter ingredients to form a thick batter.
- Spread a layer of the batter on each colocasia leaf to cover it completely.
- Place 5 coated leaves one above the other.
- Fold the leaves 2.5cm/1in from each corner to form a square. Roll this square into a cylinder.
- Repeat for the other 5 leaves.
- Steam the rolls for about 20-25 minutes. Set aside to cool.
- Slice each roll into pinwheel-like shapes. Set aside.
- Heat the oil in a saucepan. Add the mustard, sesame seeds, cumin seeds and curry leaves. Let them splutter for 15 seconds.
- Pour this over the pinwheels.
- Garnish with the coriander leaves. Serve hot.

Nargisi Chicken Kebab

(Chicken and Cheese Kebab)

Makes 20-25

Ingredients

500g/1lb 2oz chicken, minced

150g/5½oz grated Cheddar cheese

2 large onions, finely chopped

1 tsp ginger paste

1 tsp garlic paste

1 tsp ground cardamom

2 tsp garam masala

1 tsp ground coriander

½ tsp turmeric

½ tsp chilli powder

Salt to taste

15-20 raisins

Refined vegetable oil for deep frying

Method

- Knead all the ingredients, except the raisins and oil, into a dough.

- Make small dumplings. Place a raisin in the centre of each dumpling.

- Heat the oil in a frying pan. Fry the dumplings on a medium heat till golden brown. Serve hot with mint chutney

Sev Puris with Savoury Topping

Serves 4

Ingredients

24 sev puris*

2 potatoes, diced and boiled

1 large onion, finely chopped

¼ small unripe green mango, finely chopped

120ml/4fl oz hot and sour chutney

4 tbsp mint chutney

1 tsp chaat masala*

Juice of 1 lemon

Salt to taste

150g/5½oz sev*

2 tbsp coriander leaves, chopped

Method

- Arrange the puris on a serving plate.
- Place small portions of the potatoes, onion and mango on each puri.
- Sprinkle the hot and sour chutney and mint chutney on top of each puri.
- Sprinkle the chaat masala, lemon juice and salt on top.
- Garnish with the sev and coriander leaves. Serve immediately.

Special Roll

Makes 4

Ingredients

1 tsp yeast

Pinch of sugar

240ml/8fl oz warm water

350g/12oz plain white flour

½ tsp baking powder

2 tbsp butter

1 large onion, finely chopped

2 tomatoes, finely chopped

30g/1oz mint leaves, finely chopped

200g/7oz spinach, boiled

300g/10oz paneer*, diced

Salt to taste

Ground black pepper to taste

125g/4½oz tomato purée

1 egg, whisked

Method

- Dissolve the yeast and sugar in the water.
- Sieve the flour and baking powder together. Mix with the yeast and knead into a dough.
- With a rolling pin, roll out the dough into 2 chapattis. Set aside.
- Heat half the butter in a saucepan. Add the onion, tomatoes, mint leaves, spinach, paneer, salt and black pepper. Sauté on a medium heat for 3 minutes.
- Spread this over 1 chapatti. Pour the tomato purée on top and cover with the other chapatti. Seal the ends.
- Brush the chapattis with the egg and remaining butter.
- Bake in an oven at 150ºC (300ºF, Gas Mark 2) for 10 minutes. Serve hot.

Fried Colocasia

Serves 4

Ingredients

500g/1lb 2 oz colocasia*

2 tbsp ground coriander

1 tbsp ground cumin

1 tbsp amchoor*

2 tsp besan*

Salt to taste

Refined vegetable oil for frying

Chaat masala*, to taste

1 tbsp coriander leaves, chopped

½ tsp lemon juice

Method

- Boil the colocasia in a saucepan for 15 minutes on a low heat. Cool, peel, cut lengthways and flatten. Set aside.
- Mix the ground coriander, ground cumin, amchoor, besan and salt. Roll the colocasia pieces in this mixture. Set aside.
- Heat the oil in a saucepan. Deep fry the colocasia till crisp, then drain.
- Sprinkle with the remaining ingredients. Serve hot.

Mixed Dhal Dosa

(Mixed Lentil Crêpe)

Makes 8-10

Ingredients

250g/9oz rice, soaked for 5-6 hours

100g/3½oz mung dhal*, soaked for 5-6 hours

100g/3½oz chana dhal*, soaked for 5-6 hours

100g/3½oz urad dhal*, soaked for 5-6 hours

2 tbsp yoghurt

½ tsp bicarbonate of soda

2 tbsp refined vegetable oil plus extra for frying

Salt to taste

Method

- Wet grind the rice and the dhals separately. Mix together. Add the yoghurt, bicarbonate of soda, oil and salt. Whisk till fluffy and light. Set aside for 3-4 hours.
- Grease and heat a flat pan. Pour 2 tbsp of batter over it and spread like a crêpe. Pour some oil around the edges. Cook for 2 minutes. Serve hot.

Makkai Cakes

(Corn Cakes)

Makes 12-15

Ingredients

4 fresh corn cobs

2 tbsp butter

750ml/1¼ pints milk

½ tsp chilli powder

Salt to taste

Ground black pepper to taste

25g/scant 1oz coriander leaves, chopped

50g/1¾oz breadcrumbs

Method

- Remove the kernels from the corn cobs and grind them coarsely.
- Heat the butter in a saucepan and fry the ground corn for 2-3 minutes on a medium heat. Add the milk and simmer till dry.
- Add the chilli powder, salt, black pepper and coriander leaves.
- Add the breadcrumbs and mix well. Divide the mixture into small patties.
- Heat the butter in a frying pan. Shallow fry the patties till golden brown. Serve hot with ketchup.

Hara Bhara Kebab

(Green Vegetable Kebab)

Serves 4

Ingredients

300g/10oz chana dhal*, soaked overnight

2 green cardamom pods

2.5cm/1in cinnamon

Salt to taste

60ml/2fl oz water

200g/7oz spinach, steamed and ground

½ tsp garam masala

¼ tsp mace, grated

Refined vegetable oil to shallow fry

Method

- Drain the dhal. Add the cardamom, cloves, cinnamon, salt and water. Cook in a saucepan on a medium heat till soft. Grind to a paste.
- Add all the remaining ingredients, except the oil. Mix well. Divide the mixture into lemon-sized balls and flatten each into small patties.

- Heat the oil in a frying pan. Shallow fry the patties over a medium heat till golden brown. Serve hot with mint chutney

Fish Pakoda

(Battered Fried Fish)

Makes 12

Ingredients

300g/10oz boneless fish, chopped into 2.5cm/1in pieces

Salt to taste

2 tsp lemon juice

3 tbsp water

250g/9oz besan*

1 tsp garlic paste

2 green chillies, finely chopped

1 tsp garam masala

½ tsp turmeric

Refined vegetable oil for deep frying

Method

- Marinate the fish with the salt and lemon juice for 20 minutes.

- Mix the remaining ingredients, except the oil, to make a thick batter.

- Heat the oil in a saucepan. Dip each piece of fish in the batter and fry till golden. Drain on absorbent paper. Serve hot.

Shammi Kebab

(Mince and Bengal Gram Kebab)

Makes 35

Ingredients

750g/1lb 10oz chicken, minced

600g/1lb 5oz chana dhal*

3 large onions, chopped

1 tsp ginger paste

1 tsp garlic paste

2.5cm/1in cinnamon

4 cloves

2 black cardamom pods

7 peppercorns

1 tsp ground cumin

Salt to taste

450ml/15fl oz water

2 eggs, whisked

Refined vegetable oil for frying

Method

- Mix together all the ingredients, except the eggs and oil. Boil in a saucepan till all the water evaporates. Grind to a thick paste.
- Add the eggs to the paste. Mix well. Divide the mixture into 35 patties.
- Heat the oil in a frying pan. Fry the patties on a low heat till golden.
- Serve hot with mint chutney

Basic Dhokla

(Basic Steamed Cake)

Makes 18-20

Ingredients

250g/9oz rice

450g/1lb chana dhal*

60g/2oz yoghurt

¼ tsp bicarbonate of soda

6 green chillies, chopped

1cm/½in root ginger, grated

¼ tsp ground coriander

¼ tsp ground cumin

½ tsp turmeric

Salt to taste

½ coconut, grated

150g/5½oz coriander leaves, finely chopped

1 tbsp refined vegetable oil

½ tsp mustard seeds

Method

- Soak the rice and dhal together for 6 hours. Grind coarsely.
- Add the yoghurt and bicarbonate of soda. Mix well. Let the paste ferment for 6-8 hours.
- Add the green chillies, ginger, ground coriander, ground cumin, turmeric and salt to the batter. Mix thoroughly.
- Pour into a 20cm/8in round cake tin. Steam the batter for 10 minutes.
- Cool and chop into square pieces. Sprinkle the grated coconut and coriander leaves over them. Set aside.
- Heat the oil in a saucepan. Add the mustard seeds. Let them splutter for 15 seconds.
- Pour this over the dhoklas. Serve hot.

Adai

(Rice and Lentil Crêpe)

Makes 12

Ingredients

125g/4½oz rice

75g/2½oz urad dhal*

75g/2½oz chana dhal*

75g/2½oz masoor dhal*

75g/2½oz mung dhal*

6 red chillies

Salt to taste

240ml/8fl oz water

Refined vegetable oil for greasing

Method

- Soak the rice with all the dhals overnight.
- Drain the mixture and add the red chillies, salt and water. Grind until smooth.
- Grease and heat a flat pan. Spread 3 tbsp of the batter on it. Cover and cook on a medium heat for 2-3 minutes. Flip and cook the other side.
- Remove carefully with a spatula. Repeat for the rest of the batter. Serve hot.

Double Decker Dhokla

(Steamed Double Decker Cake)

Makes 20

Ingredients

500g/1lb 2oz rice

300g/10oz urad beans*

75g/2½oz urad dhal*

75g/2½oz chana dhal*

75g/2½oz masoor dhal*

2 green chillies

500g/1lb 2oz yoghurt

1 tsp chilli powder

½ tsp turmeric

Salt to taste

115g/4oz mint chutney

Method

- Mix the rice and urad beans. Soak overnight.
- Mix all the dhals. Soak overnight.
- Drain and grind the rice mixture and the dhal mixture separately. Set aside.
- Mix the green chillies, yoghurt, chilli powder, turmeric and salt together. Add half of this blend to the rice mixture and add the remaining to the dhal mixture. Allow to ferment for 6 hours.
- Grease a 20cm/8in round cake tin. Pour the rice mixture into it. Sprinkle the mint chutney on top of the rice mixture. Pour the dhal mixture on top.
- Steam for 7-8 minutes. Chop and serve hot.

Ulundu Vada

(Fried Doughnut-shaped Snack)

Makes 12

Ingredients

600g/1lb 5oz urad dhal*, soaked overnight and drained

4 green chillies, finely chopped

Salt to taste

3 tbsp water

Refined vegetable oil for deep frying

Method

- Grind the dhal with the green chillies, salt and water.
- Shape the mixture into doughnuts.
- Heat the oil in a saucepan. Add the vadas and deep fry on a medium heat till brown.
- Drain on absorbent paper. Serve hot with coconut chutney

Bhakar Wadi

(Spicy Gram Flour Pinwheel)

Serves 4

Ingredients

500g/1lb 2oz besan*

175g/6oz wholemeal flour

Salt to taste

Pinch of asafoetida

120ml/4fl oz warm refined vegetable oil plus extra for deep frying

100g/3½oz desiccated coconut

1 tsp sesame seeds

1 tsp poppy seeds

Pinch of sugar

1 tsp chilli powder

25g/scant 1oz coriander leaves, finely chopped

1 tbsp tamarind paste

Method

- Knead the besan, flour, salt, asafoetida, warm oil and enough water into a stiff dough. Set aside.

- Dry roast the coconut, sesame seeds and poppy seeds for 3-5 minutes. Grind to a powder.
- Add the sugar, salt, chilli powder, coriander leaves and tamarind paste to the powder and mix thoroughly to prepare the filling. Set aside.
- Divide the dough into lemon-sized balls. Roll each into a thin disc.
- Spread the filling on each disc so that the filling covers the entire disc. Roll each into a tight cylinder. Seal the edges with a little water.
- Slice the cylinders to get pinwheel-like shapes.
- Heat the oil in a saucepan. Add the pinwheel rolls and fry on a medium heat till crisp.
- Drain on absorbent paper. Store in an airtight container once cooled.

NOTE: These can be stored for a fortnight.

Mangalorean Chaat

Serves 4

Ingredients

75g/2½oz chana dhal*

240ml/8fl oz water

Salt to taste

Large pinch of bicarbonate of soda

2 large potatoes, finely chopped and boiled

350g/12oz fresh yoghurt

2 tbsp caster sugar

4 tbsp refined vegetable oil

1 tbsp dried fenugreek leaves

1 tsp ginger paste

1 tsp garlic paste

2 green chillies

1 tsp ground cumin, dry roasted

1 tsp garam masala

1 tbsp amchoor*

1 tsp turmeric

½ tsp chilli powder

150g/5½oz canned chickpeas

1 large onion, finely chopped

2 tbsp coriander leaves, finely chopped

Method

- Cook the dhal with the water, salt and bicarbonate of soda in a saucepan on a medium heat for 30 minutes. Add more water if the dhal feels too dry. Mix the potatoes with the dhal mixture and set aside.
- Whisk the yoghurt with the sugar. Place in the freezer to chill.
- Heat the oil in a saucepan. Add the fenugreek leaves and fry on a medium heat for 3-4 minutes.
- Add the ginger paste, garlic paste, green chillies, ground cumin, garam masala, amchoor, turmeric and chilli powder. Fry for 2-3 minutes, stirring continuously.
- Add the chickpeas. Sauté for 5 minutes, stirring continuously. Add the dhal mixture and mix well.
- Remove from the heat and spread the mixture on a serving platter.
- Pour the sweet yoghurt on top.
- Sprinkle with the onion and coriander leaves. Serve immediately.

Pani Puri

Makes 30

Ingredients
For the puris:

175g/6oz plain white flour

100g/3½oz semolina

Salt to taste

Refined vegetable oil for deep frying

For the stuffing:

50g/1¾oz sprouted mung beans

150g/5½oz sprouted chickpeas

Salt to taste

2 large potatoes, boiled and mashed

For the pani:

2 tbsp tamarind paste

100g/3½oz coriander leaves, finely chopped

1½ tsp ground cumin, dry roasted

2-4 green chillies, finely chopped

2.5cm/1in root ginger

Rock salt to taste

240ml/8fl oz water

Method

- Knead all the puri ingredients, except the oil, with enough water to form a stiff dough.
- Roll out into small puris of 5cm/2in diameter.
- Heat the oil in a frying pan. Deep fry the puris till light brown. Set aside.
- For the stuffing, parboil the sprouted mung beans and chickpeas with the salt. Mix with the potatoes. Set aside.
- For the pani, grind together all the pani ingredients, except the water.
- Add this mixture to the water. Mix well and set aside.
- To serve, make a hole in each puri and fill it with the stuffing. Pour 3 tbsp of the pani into each and serve immediately.

Stuffed Spinach Egg

Serves 4

Ingredients

200g/7oz spinach

Pinch of bicarbonate of soda

1 tbsp refined vegetable oil

1 tsp cumin seeds

6 garlic cloves, crushed

2 green chillies, ground

Salt to taste

8 hard boiled eggs, halved lengthways

1 tbsp ghee

1 onion, finely chopped

2.5cm/1in root ginger, chopped

Method

- Mix the spinach with the bicarbonate of soda. Steam till tender. Grind and set aside.
- Heat the oil in a saucepan. When it begins to smoke, add the cumin seeds, garlic and green chillies. Stir-fry for a few seconds. Add the steamed spinach and salt.
- Cover with a lid and cook till dry. Set aside.
- Scoop the yolks out from the eggs. Add the egg yolks to the spinach mixture. Mix well.
- Place spoonfuls of the spinach-egg mixture in the hollow egg whites. Set aside.
- Heat the ghee in a small frying pan. Fry the onion and ginger till golden brown.
- Sprinkle this on top of the eggs. Serve hot.

Sada Dosa

(Savoury Rice Crêpe)

Makes 15

Ingredients

100g/3½oz parboiled rice

75g/2½oz urad dhal*

½ tsp fenugreek seeds

½ tsp bicarbonate of soda

Salt to taste

125g/4½oz yoghurt, whipped

60ml/2fl oz refined vegetable oil

Method

- Soak the rice and the dhal together with the fenugreek seeds for 7-8 hours.
- Drain and grind the mixture to a grainy paste.
- Add bicarbonate of soda and salt. Mix well.
- Set aside to ferment for 8-10 hours.
- Add the yoghurt to make the batter. This batter should be thick enough to coat a spoon. Add a little water if needed. Set aside.

- Grease and heat a flat pan. Spread a spoonful of the batter over it to make a thin crêpe. Pour 1 tsp oil on top. Cook until crisp. Repeat for the rest of the batter and serve hot.

Potato Samosa

(Potato Savoury)

Makes 20

Ingredients

175g/6oz plain white flour

Pinch of salt

5 tbsp refined vegetable oil plus extra for deep frying

100ml/3½fl oz water

1cm/½in root ginger, grated

2 green chillies, finely chopped

2 garlic cloves, finely chopped

½ tsp ground coriander

1 large onion, finely chopped

2 large potatoes, boiled and mashed

1 tbsp coriander leaves, finely chopped

1 tbsp lemon juice

½ tsp turmeric

1 tsp chilli powder

½ tsp garam masala

Salt to taste

Method

- Mix the flour with the salt, 2 tbsp oil and water. Knead into a pliable dough.
  Cover with a moist cloth and set aside for 15-20 minutes.
- Knead the dough again. Cover with a moist cloth and set aside.
- For the filling, heat 3 tbsp oil in a frying pan. Add the ginger, green chillies, garlic and ground coriander. Fry for a minute on a medium heat, stirring continuously.
- Add the onion and fry till brown.
- Add the potatoes, coriander leaves, lemon juice, turmeric, chilli powder, garam masala and salt. Mix thoroughly.
- Cook on a low heat for 4 minutes, stirring occasionally. Set aside.
- To make the samosas, divide the dough into 10 balls. Roll out into discs of 12cm/5in diameter. Cut each disc into 2 half-moons.
- Run a moist finger along the diameter of a half-moon. Bring the ends together to make a cone.
- Place a tbsp of the filling in the cone and seal by pressing the edges together. Repeat for all the half-moons.
- Heat the oil in a frying pan. Deep fry the samosas, five at a time, over a low heat till light brown. Drain on absorbent paper.
- Serve hot with mint chutney

Hot Kachori

(Fried Dumpling with Lentil Filling)

Makes 15

Ingredients

250g/9oz plain white flour plus 1 tbsp for the patching

5 tbsp refined vegetable oil plus extra for deep frying

Salt to taste

1.4 litres/2½ pints water plus 1 tbsp for patching

300g/10oz mung dhal*, soaked for 30 minutes

½ tsp ground coriander

½ tsp ground fennel

½ tsp cumin seeds

½ tsp mustard seeds

2-3 pinches of asafoetida

1 tsp garam masala

1 tsp chilli powder

Method

- Mix 250g/9oz flour with 3 tbsp oil, salt and 100ml/3½fl oz of the water. Knead into a soft, pliable dough. Set aside for 30 minutes.

- To make the filling, cook the dhal with the remaining water in a saucepan on a medium heat for 45 minutes. Drain and set aside.

- Heat 2 tbsp oil in a saucepan. When it begins to smoke, add the ground coriander, fennel, cumin seeds, mustard seeds, asafoetida, garam masala, chilli powder and salt. Let them splutter for 30 seconds.

- Add the cooked dhal. Mix well and fry for 2-3 minutes, stirring continuously.

- Cool the dhal mixture and divide into 15 lemon-sized balls. Set aside.

- Mix 1 tbsp flour with 1 tbsp water to make a paste for patching. Set aside.

- Divide the dough into 15 balls. Roll out into discs of 12cm/5in diameter.

- Place 1 ball of the filling in the centre of a disc. Seal like a pouch.

- Flatten slightly by pressing it between the palms. Repeat for the remaining discs.

- Heat the oil in a saucepan until it starts smoking. Deep fry the discs till golden brown on the underside. Flip and repeat.

- If a kachori tears while frying, seal it with the patching paste.

- Drain on absorbent paper. Serve hot with mint chutney

Khandvi

(Besan Roll-Ups)

Makes 10-15

Ingredients

60g/2oz besan*

60g/2oz yoghurt

120ml/4fl oz water

1 tsp turmeric

Salt to taste

5 tbsp refined vegetable oil

1 tbsp fresh coconut, grated

1 tbsp coriander leaves, finely chopped

½ tsp mustard seeds

2 pinches of asafoetida

8 curry leaves

2 green chillies, finely chopped

1 tsp sesame seeds

Method

- Mix the besan, yoghurt, water, turmeric and salt together.
- Heat 4 tbsp oil in a frying pan. Add the besan mixture and cook, stirring continuously to make sure no lumps are formed.
- Cook till the mixture leaves the sides of the pan. Set aside.
- Grease two 15 × 35cm/6 × 14in non-stick baking trays. Pour in the besan mixture and smooth flat with a palette knife. Allow to set for 10 minutes.
- Cut the mixture into 5cm/2in wide strips. Carefully roll up each strip.
- Place the rolls in a serving dish. Sprinkle the grated coconut and coriander leaves on top. Set aside.
- Heat 1 tbsp oil in a small saucepan. Add the mustard seeds, asafoetida, curry leaves, green chillies and sesame seeds. Let them splutter for 15 seconds.
- Pour this immediately over the besan rolls. Serve hot or at room temperature.

Makkai Squares

(Corn Squares)

Makes 12

Ingredients

2 tsp ghee

100g/3½oz corn kernels, ground

Salt to taste

125g/4½oz boiled peas

3 tbsp refined vegetable oil

8 green chillies, finely chopped

½ tsp cumin seeds

½ tsp mustard seeds

½ tsp garlic paste

½ tbsp ground coriander

½ tbsp ground cumin

175g/6oz maize flour

175g/6oz wholemeal flour

150ml/5fl oz water

Method

- Heat the ghee in a saucepan. When it begins to smoke, fry the corn for 3 minutes. Set aside.
- Add salt to the boiled peas. Mash the peas well. Set aside.
- Heat 2 tbsp oil in a frying pan. Add the green chillies, cumin and mustard seeds. Let them splutter for 15 seconds.
- Add the fried corn, mashed peas, garlic paste, ground coriander and ground cumin. Mix well. Remove from the heat and set aside.
- Mix both the flours together. Add salt and 1 tbsp oil. Add the water and knead into a soft dough.
- Roll out 24 square shapes, each square 10x10cm/4x4in in size.
- Place the corn and peas mixture in the centre of a square and cover with another square. Gently press the edges of the square to seal.
- Repeat for the rest of the squares.
- Grease and heat a frying pan. Roast the squares on the pan till golden brown.
- Serve hot with ketchup.

Dhal Pakwan

(Crispy Bread with Lentils)

Serves 4

Ingredients

600g/1lb 5oz chana dhal*

3 tbsp refined vegetable oil

1 tsp cumin seeds

750ml/1¼ pints water

Salt to taste

½ tsp turmeric

½ tsp amchoor*

10g/¼oz coriander leaves, finely chopped

For the pakwan:

250g/9oz plain white flour

½ tsp cumin seeds

Salt to taste

Refined vegetable oil for deep frying

Method

- Soak the chana dhal for 4 hours. Drain and set aside.
- Heat the oil in a saucepan. Add the cumin seeds. Let them splutter for 15 seconds.
- Add the soaked dhal, water, salt and turmeric. Simmer for 30 minutes.
- Transfer to a serving dish. Sprinkle with the amchoor and coriander leaves. Set aside.
- Knead all the pakwan ingredients, except the oil, with enough water to make a stiff dough.
- Divide into walnut-sized balls. Roll out into thick discs, 10cm/4in in diameter. Pierce all over with a fork.
- Heat the oil in a frying pan. Deep fry the discs till golden. Drain on absorbent paper.
- Serve the pakwans with the hot dhal.

Spicy Sev

(Spicy Gram Flour Flakes)

Serves 4

Ingredients

500g/1lb 2oz besan*

1 tsp ajowan seeds

1 tbsp refined vegetable oil plus extra for deep frying

¼ tsp asafoetida

Salt to taste

200ml/7fl oz water

Method

- Knead the besan with the ajowan seeds, oil, asafoetida, salt and water into a sticky dough.
- Put the dough in a piping bag.
- Heat the oil in a saucepan. Press the dough through the nozzle in the form of noodles into the pan and fry lightly on both sides.
- Drain well and cool before storing.

NOTE: *This can be stored for a fortnight.*

Stuffed Veggie Crescents

Makes 6

Ingredients

350g/12oz plain white flour

6 tbsp warm refined vegetable oil plus extra for deep frying

Salt to taste

1 tomato, sliced

For the filling:

3 tbsp refined vegetable oil

200g/7oz peas

1 carrot, julienned

100g/3½oz French beans, chopped into thin strips

4 tbsp fresh coconut, grated

3 green chillies

2.5cm/1in root ginger, crushed

4 tsp coriander leaves, finely chopped

2 tsp sugar

2 tsp lemon juice

Salt to taste

Method

- First make the filling. Heat the oil in a saucepan. Add the peas, carrot and French beans and fry, stirring continuously, till soft.
- Add all the remaining filling ingredients and mix well. Set aside.
- Mix the flour with the oil and the salt. Knead into a stiff dough.
- Divide the dough into 6 lemon-sized balls.
- Roll each ball into a disc of 10cm/4in diameter.
- Place the vegetable filling on one half of a disc. Fold the other half over to cover the filling and press the edges together to seal.
- Repeat for all the discs.
- Heat the oil in a saucepan. Add the crescents and fry till they are golden brown.
- Arrange them in a round serving dish and garnish with the tomato slices. Serve immediately.

Kachori Usal

(Fried Bread with Chickpeas)

Serves 4

Ingredients
For the pastry:

50g/1¾oz fenugreek leaves finely chopped

175g/6oz wholemeal flour

2 green chillies, finely chopped

1 tsp ginger paste

¼ tsp turmeric

100ml/3½fl oz water

Salt to taste

For the filling:

1 tsp refined vegetable oil

250g/9oz mung beans, boiled

250g/9oz green chickpeas, boiled

¼ tsp turmeric

½ tsp chilli powder

1 tsp ground coriander

1 tsp ground cumin

Salt to taste

For the sauce:

2 tsp refined vegetable oil

2 large onions, finely chopped

2 tomatoes, chopped

1 tsp garlic paste

½ tsp garam masala

¼ tsp chilli powder

Salt to taste

Method

- Mix all the pastry ingredients together. Knead into a firm dough. Set aside.
- For the filling, heat the oil in a frying pan and sauté all the filling ingredients on a medium heat for 5 minutes. Set aside.
- For the sauce, heat the oil in a frying pan. Add all the sauce ingredients. Fry for 5 minutes, stirring occasionally. Set aside.
- Divide the dough into 8 portions. Roll out each portion into a disc of 10cm/4in diameter.
- Place some filling in the centre of a disc. Seal like a pouch and smooth to form a stuffed ball. Repeat for all the discs.

- Steam the balls for 15 minutes.
- Add the balls to the sauce and toss to coat. Cook on a low heat for 5 minutes.
- Serve hot.

Dhal Dhokli

(Gujarati Savoury Snack)

Serves 4

Ingredients
For the dhokli:

175g/6oz wholemeal flour

Pinch of turmeric

¼ tsp chilli powder

½ tsp ajowan seeds

1 tsp refined vegetable oil

100ml/3½fl oz water

For the dhal:

2 tbsp refined vegetable oil

3-4 cloves

5cm/2in cinnamon

1 tsp mustard seeds

300g/10oz masoor dhal*, cooked and mashed

½ tsp turmeric

Pinch of asafoetida

1 tbsp tamarind paste

2 tbsp grated jaggery*

60g/2oz peanuts

1 tsp ground coriander

1 tsp ground cumin

½ tsp chilli powder

Salt to taste

25g/scant 1oz coriander leaves, finely chopped

Method

- Mix all the dhokli ingredients together. Knead to form a firm dough.
- Divide the dough into 5-6 balls. Roll out into thick discs, 6cm/2.4in in diameter. Set aside for 10 minutes to harden.
- Cut out the dhokli discs into diamond-shaped pieces. Set aside.
- For the dhal, heat the oil in a saucepan. Add the cloves, cinnamon and mustard seeds. Let them splutter for 15 seconds.
- Add all the remaining dhal ingredients, except the coriander leaves. Mix well. Cook on a high heat till the dhal starts boiling.
- Add the dhokli pieces to the boiling dhal. Continue to cook over a low heat for 10 minutes.
- Garnish with the coriander leaves. Serve hot.

Misal

(Healthy Sprouted Beans Snack)

Serves 4

Ingredients

3-4 tbsp refined vegetable oil

½ tsp mustard seeds

¼ tsp asafoetida

6 curry leaves

1 tsp ginger paste

1 tsp garlic paste

25g/scant 1oz coriander leaves, ground in a blender

1 tsp chilli powder

1 tsp tamarind paste

2 tsp grated jaggery*

Salt to taste

300g/10oz sprouted mung beans, boiled

2 large potatoes, diced and boiled

500ml/16fl oz water

300g/10oz Bombay Mix*

1 large tomato, finely chopped

1 large onion, finely chopped

25g/scant 1oz coriander leaves, finely chopped

4 slices of bread

For the spice mixture:

1 tsp cumin seeds

2 tsp coriander seeds

2 cloves

3 peppercorns

¼ tsp ground cinnamon

Method

- Grind together all the ingredients of the spice mixture. Set aside.
- Heat the oil in a saucepan. Add the mustard seeds, asafoetida and curry leaves. Let them splutter for 2-3 minutes.
- Add the ginger paste, garlic paste, ground coriander leaves, chilli powder, tamarind paste, jaggery and salt. Mix well and cook for 3-4 minutes.
- Add the ground spice mixture. Sauté for 2-3 minutes.
- Add the sprouted beans, potatoes and water. Mix well and simmer for 15 minutes.
- Transfer to a serving bowl and sprinkle with the Bombay Mix, chopped tomato, chopped onion and coriander leaves on top.
- Serve hot with a slice of bread on the side.

Pandori

(Mung Dhal Snack)

Ingredients

1 green chilli, halved lengthways

Salt to taste

1 tsp bicarbonate of soda

¼ tsp asafoetida

250g/9oz whole mung dhal*, soaked for 4 hours

2 tsp refined vegetable oil

2 tsp coriander leaves, finely chopped

Method

- Add the green chilli, salt, bicarbonate of soda and asafoetida to the dhal. Grind to a paste.
- Grease a 20cm/8in round cake tin with the oil and pour the dhal paste in it. Steam for 10 minutes.
- Set the steamed dhal mixture aside for 10 minutes. Once cool, cut into 2.5cm/1in pieces.
- Garnish with the coriander leaves. Serve hot with green coconut chutney

Vegetable Adai

(Vegetable, Rice and Lentil Crêpe)

Makes 8

Ingredients

100g/3½oz parboiled rice

150g/5½oz masoor dhal*

75g/2½oz urad dhal*

3-4 red chillies

¼ tsp asafoetida

Salt to taste

4 tbsp water

1 onion, finely chopped

½ carrot, finely chopped

50g/1¾oz cabbage,

finely chopped 4-5 curry leaves

10g/¼oz coriander leaves, finely chopped

4 tsp refined vegetable oil

Method

- Soak the rice and the dhals together for about 20 minutes.
- Drain and add the red chillies, asafoetida, salt and water. Grind to a coarse paste.
- Add the onion, carrot, cabbage, curry leaves and coriander leaves. Mix well to make a batter with a consistency similar to sponge cake batter. Add more water if the consistency is not right.
- Grease a flat pan. Pour a spoonful of the batter. Spread with the back of a spoon to make a thin crêpe.
- Pour half a tsp oil around the crêpe. Flip to cook both sides.
- Repeat for the rest of the batter. Serve hot with coconut chutney

Spicy Corn on the Cob

Serves 4

Ingredients

8 corn cobs

Salted butter to taste

Salt to taste

2 tsp chaat masala[*]

2 lemons, halved

Method

- Roast the corns cobs on a charcoal grill or open flame till golden brown all over.
- Rub the butter, salt, chaat masala and the lemons on each cob.
- Serve immediately.

Mixed Vegetable Chop

Makes 12

Ingredients

Salt to taste

¼ tsp ground black pepper

4-5 large potatoes, boiled and mashed

2 tbsp refined vegetable oil plus extra for deep frying

1 small onion, finely chopped

½ tsp garam masala

1 tsp lemon juice

100g/3½oz frozen mixed vegetables

2-3 green chillies, finely chopped

50g/1¾oz coriander leaves, finely chopped

250g/9oz arrowroot powder

150ml/5fl oz water

100g/3½oz breadcrumbs

Method

- Add the salt and black pepper to the potatoes. Mix well and divide into 12 balls. Set aside.
- For the filling, heat 2 tbsp oil in a frying pan. Fry the onion on a medium heat till translucent.
- Add the garam masala, lemon juice, mixed vegetables, green chillies and coriander leaves. Mix well and cook on a medium heat for 2-3 minutes. Mash well and set aside.
- Flatten the potato balls with greased palms.
- Place some filling mixture on eacn potato patty. Seal to make oblong-shaped chops. Set aside.
- Mix the arrowroot powder with enough water to form a thin batter.
- Heat the oil in a frying pan. Dip the chops in the batter, roll in the breadcrumbs and deep fry on a medium heat till golden brown.
- Drain and serve hot.

Idli Upma

(Steamed Rice Cake Snack)

Serves 4

Ingredients

5 tbsp refined vegetable oil

½ tsp mustard seeds

½ tsp cumin seeds

1 tsp urad dhal*

2 green chillies, slit lengthways

8 curry leaves

Pinch of asafoetida

¼ tsp turmeric

8 idlis crushed

2 tsp caster sugar

1 tbsp coriander leaves, finely chopped

Salt to taste

Method

- Heat the oil in a saucepan. Add the mustard seeds, cumin seeds, urad dhal, green chillies, curry leaves, asafoetida and turmeric. Let them splutter for 30 seconds.
- Add the crushed idlis, caster sugar, coriander and salt. Mix gently.
- Serve immediately.

Dhal Bhajiya

(Batter Fried Lentil Balls)

Makes 15

Ingredients

250/9oz mung dhal*, soaked for 2-3 hours

2 green chillies, finely chopped

2 tbsp coriander leaves, finely chopped

1 tsp cumin seeds

Salt to taste

Refined vegetable oil for deep frying

Method

- Drain the dhal and grind coarsely.
- Add the chillies, coriander leaves, cumin seeds and salt. Mix well.
- Heat the oil in a frying pan. Add small portions of the dhal mixture and fry over a medium heat till golden brown.
- Serve hot with mint chutney

Masala Papad

(Poppadoms Topped with Spices)

Makes 8

Ingredients

2 tomatoes, finely chopped

2 large onions, finely chopped

3 green chillies, finely chopped

10g/¼oz coriander leaves, chopped

2 tsp lemon juice

1 tsp chaat masala*

Salt to taste

8 poppadoms

Method

- Mix all the ingredients, except the poppadoms, in a bowl.
- Roast the poppadoms on a high heat, turning each side. Make sure you don't burn them.
- Spread the vegetable mixture over each poppadom. Serve immediately.

Vegetable Sandwich

Makes 6

Ingredients

12 bread slices

50g/1¾oz butter

100g/3½oz mint chutney

1 large potato, boiled and thinly sliced

1 tomato, thinly sliced

1 large onion, thinly sliced

1 cucumber, thinly sliced

Chaat masala* to taste

Salt to taste

Method

- Butter the bread slices and apply a thin coat of mint chutney on each.
- Place a layer of potato, tomato, onion and cucumber slices on 6 bread slices.
- Sprinkle with some chaat masala and salt.
- Cover with the remaining bread slices and cut as desired. Serve immediately.

Paneer Salad

Serves 4

Ingredients

1 green pepper, diced

1 large onion, finely chopped

125g/4½oz pomegranate seeds

3 tsp chaat masala*

10g/¼oz coriander leaves, finely chopped

2 tsp lemon juice

Salt to taste

500g/1lb 2oz paneer*,

diced

Method

- In a bowl, mix all the ingredients thoroughly, except the paneer.
- Add the paneer pieces gently, making sure they do not crumble. Mix carefully.
- Serve chilled.

Corn Salad

Serves 24

Ingredients

2 tsp refined vegetable oil

½ tsp cumin seeds

1 large onion, finely chopped

2 green chillies, finely chopped

1 tomato, finely chopped

400g/14oz boiled corn kernels

Salt to taste

2 tsp lemon juice

1 tsp chaat masala*

1 tbsp coriander leaves, finely chopped

Method

- Heat the oil in a saucepan. Add the cumin seeds. Let them splutter for 15 seconds.
- Add the onion and fry for a minute.
- Add the chillies, tomato, corn and salt. Cook for a minute, stirring continuously.
- Add the lemon juice, chaat masala and coriander leaves.
- Serve at room temperature.

Stir-Fried Salad

Ingredients

2 tsp refined vegetable oil

100g/3½oz mushrooms, sliced

100g/3½oz baby corn, sliced lengthwise

1 green pepper, cored, deseeded and sliced

½ tsp ground black pepper

2 green chillies, slit lengthways

Salt to taste

1 tomato, finely sliced

1 tsp lemon juice

Method

- Heat the oil in a saucepan. Add the mushrooms, baby corn and green pepper. Stir-fry on a high heat for 2 minutes.
- Add the remaining ingredients. Cook for another minute on a medium heat. Serve warm.

Spinach Salad

Serves 4

Ingredients

200g/7oz spinach, chopped

1.5 litres/2¾ pints salted hot water

1½ tbsp clear honey

½ tbsp roasted sesame seeds

½ tbsp lemon juice

Salt to taste

Method

- Soak the spinach in the water for 2 minutes and drain completely.
- Add all the remaining ingredients to the spinach. Mix well.
- Serve chilled.

Prawn Salad

Serves 4

Ingredients

250g/9oz prawns, shelled and de-veined

Salt to taste

1 tbsp lemon juice

750 ml/1¼fl oz water

50g/1¾oz spring onions, finely chopped

10g/¼oz coriander leaves, finely chopped

3 tsp chaat masala*

2 green chillies, finely chopped

1 tomato, finely chopped

1 green pepper, finely chopped

Method

- Boil the prawns in a saucepan with the salt, lemon juice and water on a medium heat for 10 minutes. Drain and cool.
- Mix thoroughly with all the other ingredients in a bowl.
- Serve chilled.

Pineapple & Honey Raita

Serves 4

Ingredients

250g/9oz pineapple, diced

85g/3oz mixed nuts (cashew nuts, pistachios and walnuts)

1 tsp honey

450g/1lb yoghurt

Salt to taste

Method

- Mix all the ingredients together in a bowl.
- Serve chilled.

Mango Raita

Serves 4

Ingredients

450g/1lb ripe mangoes, peeled and diced

450g/1lb yoghurt

¼ tsp saffron, soaked in 1 tbsp milk

Salt to taste

Method

- Mix all the ingredients together in a bowl.
- Serve chilled.

Apple Walnut Raita

Serves 4

Ingredients

2 apples, cored and diced

85g/3oz walnuts, chopped

350g/12oz yoghurt

Salt to taste

Method

- Mix all the ingredients together in a bowl.
- Serve chilled.

Bottle Gourd Raita

Serves 4

Ingredients

1 bottle gourd*, peeled and grated

350g/12oz yoghurt

½ tsp ground black pepper

1 tbsp coriander leaves, finely chopped

Salt to taste

Method

- Steam the bottle gourd till soft.
- Squeeze out the excess water and mix with the remaining ingredients. Serve chilled.

Cucumber Raita

Serves 4

Ingredients

1 large cucumber, grated

450g/1lb yoghurt

2 green chillies, slit lengthways

1 tbsp ready-made mustard

Salt to taste

Method

- Squeeze out the excess water from the cucumber.
- Add all the remaining ingredients. Mix well. Serve chilled.

Carrot Raita

Serves 4

Ingredients

2 large carrots, finely grated

450g/1lb yoghurt

2 green chillies, slit lengthways

2 tbsp roasted peanuts

1 tsp sugar (optional)

Salt to taste

Method

- Mix all the ingredients well in a bowl. Serve chilled.